Disney MOVIE MAGIC

A piano accompaniment book (HL00841181) is available for this collection.

ISBN 978-0-7935-7841-2

HAL•LEONARD®
CORPORATION
7777 W. BLUEMOUND RD. P.O. BOX 13819 MILWAUKEE, WI 53213

Visit Hal Leonard Online at
www.halleonard.com

OUT OF THIN AIR

from Walt Disney's ALADDIN AND THE KING OF THIEVES

Viola

Words and Music by
DAVID FRIEDMAN

CAN YOU FEEL THE LOVE TONIGHT

from Walt Disney Pictures' THE LION KING

Viola

Music by ELTON JOHN
Lyrics by TIM RICE

CIRCLE OF LIFE

from Walt Disney Pictures' THE LION KING

Viola

Music by ELTON JOHN
Lyrics by TIM RICE

HAKUNA MATATA

from Walt Disney Pictures' THE LION KING

Music by ELTON JOHN
Lyrics by TIM RICE

Viola

I JUST CAN'T WAIT TO BE KING

from Walt Disney Pictures' THE LION KING

Viola

Music by ELTON JOHN
Lyrics by TIM RICE

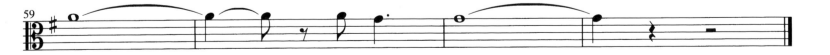

THIS LAND

from Walt Disney Pictures' THE LION KING

Music by
HANS ZIMMER

Viola

THE VIRGINIA COMPANY
from Walt Disney's POCAHONTAS

Music by ALAN MENKEN
Lyrics by STEPHEN SCHWARTZ

Viola

COLORS OF THE WIND

from Walt Disney's POCAHONTAS

Viola

Music by ALAN MENKEN
Lyrics by STEPHEN SCHWARTZ

D.S. al Coda

CODA

JUST AROUND THE RIVERBEND
from Walt Disney's POCAHONTAS

Music by ALAN MENKEN
Lyrics by STEPHEN SCHWARTZ

Viola

15

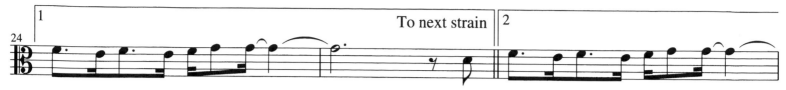

To next strain

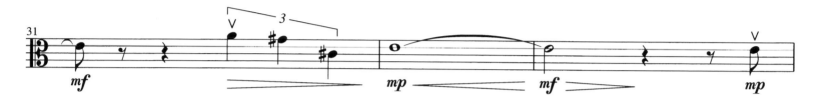

To Coda

rall.

mf   mp   mf   mp

D.S. al Coda

CODA

Meno mosso - freely

mp   rall.

Piu mosso

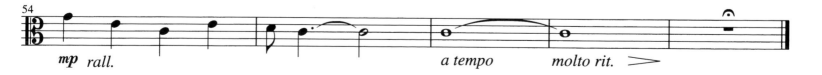

mf

mp rall.   a tempo   molto rit.

MINE, MINE, MINE
from Walt Disney's POCAHONTAS

Viola

Music by ALAN MENKEN
Lyrics by STEPHEN SCHWARTZ

CRUELLA DE VIL
from Walt Disney's 101 DALMATIANS

Words and Music by
MEL LEVEN

Viola

Moderate Swing

FORGET ABOUT LOVE
from Walt Disney's THE RETURN OF JAFAR

Words and Music by
MICHAEL SILVERSHER and PATTY SILVERSHER

Viola

Freely

YOU'VE GOT A FRIEND IN ME

from Walt Disney's TOY STORY

Viola

Music and Lyrics by
RANDY NEWMAN

STRANGE THINGS

from Walt Disney's TOY STORY

Viola

Music and Lyrics by
RANDY NEWMAN